PRAYERS
from a troubled
HEART

George Appleton

FORTRESS PRESS Philadelphia

The compiler is grateful for permission to include certain prayers which he has found particularly helpful to his own faith and devotion. The unattributed prayers are his own.

Thanks are due to the following for permission to reproduce material from copyright sources:

"The Eternal Mystery" is taken from *The Paths to Contemplation* by Yves Raguin SJ and is used by permission of the publishers, Anthony Clarke, Wheathamstead, England.

'In Suffering' from *The Pain That Heals* by Martin Israel. Copyright © 1981 by the author. Reprinted and used by permission of Hodder and Stoughton Limited and The Crossroad Publishing Company, New York.

"Feeling Lost" from *Thoughts In Solitude* by Thomas Merton. Copyright © 1956, 1958 by the Abbey of Our Lady of Gethsemani. Reprinted by permission of Farrar, Straus & Giroux, Inc.

The Sue Ryder Foundation for the sick and disabled of all ages: Prayer found in the Ravensbruck Nazi concentration camp.

"Which Way to Turn" from *One Man's Prayers* by George Appleton. (London: SPCK, 1967). © George Appleton 1967, 1977. Reprinted by permission.

"Never Enough" from *Jerusalem Prayers* by George Appleton. (London: SPCK, 1974). © George Appleton, 1974. Reprinted by permission.

The majority of Scripture quotations in this publication are from the Revised Standard Version of the Bible, copyright 1946, 1952 © 1971, 1973 by the Division of Christian Education of the National Council of the Churches of Christ in the U.S.A.

Library of Congress Cataloging in Publication Data

Appleton, George, 1902–
    Prayers from a troubled heart.

    1. Prayers. I. Title.
BV245.A623 1983   248.3'2   83–48010
ISBN 0–8006–1711–8 (pbk.)

K109D83   Printed in the United States of America   1–1711

Contents

About These Prayers

A number of friends have asked me if I could write a little book of prayers which could be used in moments of anxiety, loneliness, depression, when clouds of darkness descend on the spirit, when God seems hidden, when pain racks the body or sickness clouds the mind, when even the memory of past mercies fails to warm the heart.

I myself am old, over eighty years of age, so the prayers are very personal and real, sometimes coming from the temptations facing my own spirit, sometimes arising when people in my pastoral care have taken me into their confidence, longing for deeper faith in God and assurance of his never-failing love.

So I have prayed these prayers and written them down for my own repeated use, with the hope that they would bring to others the comfort which I have received from God.

Each prayer is linked with a verse of Scripture, and it may be that the text is more important than my prayers, for with a quiet mind and a trusting spirit the Spirit of God can speak to the troubled heart and lead it forth beside the waters of comfort. What I think I am trying to say is that God, given the opportunity, will speak in the language of the heart to everyone who has within him or her the seed of divinity, and that means everyone. We all need the spirit of the infant Samuel, who was instructed by the old priest in the very first sanctuary, in the land now called "holy"—"Speak, Lord, for your servant is listening."

So having poured out our heart to God, we need to listen, to keep our heart open both for his response and his action within us.

What I am learning is this—to memorize short prayers of love and trust so that when the conscious mind is no longer able to think or remember, the heart will pray. And when this physical, material, mortal life ends I shall already feel at home in the new and eternal order of being. This thought has been suggested by a prayer of William of Thierry, a contemplative and mystic who lived and prayed 1085–1148:

> Lord, I am a countryman,
> coming from my country to yours.
>> Teach me
>> the laws of your country
>> its ways of life
>> its spirit
> so that I may feel at home there.

In prayer the spirit moves across the frontier to the heavenly Jerusalem, which is willed by God to be the mother of us all.

November 1982   G.A.

The compiler is grateful for permission to include certain prayers which he has found particularly helpful to his own faith and devotion. The unattributed prayers are his own.

A Troubled Heart

WHEN ANXIOUS

Let nothing disturb thee,
Let nothing dismay thee:
All things pass:
God never changes.
Patience attains
All that it strives for:
He who has God
Finds he lacks nothing:
God alone suffices.

St. Teresa of Avila
(1515–82)

1 Peter 5:7

Cast all your anxieties on him, for he cares about you.

WHEN DISCOURAGED

Discouraged in the work of life,
  Disheartened by its load,
Shamed by its failures or its fear
  I sink beside the road;
But only let me think of Thee
  And then new hope springs up in me.

Samuel Longfellow (1819–92)

2 Corinthians 12:9

My grace is sufficient for you, for my power is made perfect
in weakness.

WHEN SELF-CONSCIOUS

Lord, when I am self-centered, let me look up to you and outward to other people, so that I may forget myself, but never forget you or your other children. Keep me from self-love, self-pity, self-will in every guise and disguise, and never let me measure myself by myself, but only by your Son who shows us man as you meant us to be and as we may become by your grace.

Adapted from a prayer by Eric Milner-White

Matthew 11:29

Learn from me; for I am gentle and lowly in heart, and you will find rest for your souls.

IN TIMES OF DRYNESS

O God there are times when my heart is cold and dry, when I cannot feel you near, nor find any satisfaction in prayer. At such times, O God hidden from my sight, I can only offer my will and cry out with Christ on the cross, "*My* God! *My* God! My God still!"

Psalm 42:1–2

As a [hunted] deer longs for the running brooks: so longs my soul for you O God. My soul is thirsty for God, thirsty for the living God: when shall I come and see his face?

UNDER ATTACK OR CRITICISM

O God, grant that when under attack or criticism I may stand before thee in a spirit of integrity, wanting only the truth of each situation and your will to respond to it.

O Lord, I know that I can never expect complete certainty, but can only act in faith.

I know that if I act in faith and move forward in what I believe is thy will, you can direct me and correct my course if it be wrong.

If I am paralyzed in fear, you cannot guide me.

Let me fear nothing except to be faithless to you; nor let me be consciously defensive; nor hit back on those who attack; nor become bitter or self-pitying; nor fail in the desire for truth and the expression of unfailing good will.

For the sake of him who came to bear witness to your truth and embodied your love, even Jesus Christ, my Lord.

1 Peter 2:22–23

He committed no sin; no guile was found on his lips. When he was reviled, he did not revile in return; when he suffered, he did not threaten; but trusted to him who judges justly.

WHEN TEMPTED

Dear God, I know that you do not lead me into temptation, but you are with me in every temptation to alert me to evil. I know your grace can strengthen me to resist every temptation, and that you will not allow me to be tried more than I can bear. Come to my rescue, dear Lord, stretch out your hand, as your perfect Son did to Peter sinking in the waves, and who himself resisted temptation even unto death, undefeated in trust, never failing in love.

1 Corinthians 10:13

No temptation has overtaken you that is not common to man. God is faithful and he will not let you be tempted beyond your strength, but with the temptation will also provide the way of escape, that you may be able to endure it.

IN DEPRESSION

Dear God and Father, when a thick cloud of darkness descends upon my spirit, remind me to look up in bare faith to you. I send quick darts of willed love to you: let them pierce the darkness and make a path for your love to rekindle my trembling faith and warm my lonely heart. Let me remember how your perfect Son experienced the same depths on the cross, and called out to you in undefeated faith, so he would be my beloved brother and you my ever-loving God.

Psalm 130:1, 6

Out of the deep I call to you, O Lord . . . more than they that watch for the morning.

OFTEN AFRAID

Lord God, my heart is often afraid, fearful of the future, old age, death, misfortune, loss of loved ones, failure, ill will from others. Forgive my lack of faith in you to guide and protect me. Even if the worst happens, you are always present in it, so that the feared worst cannot harm the eternal me. Nothing can snatch me out of your hand, nor from any of my loved ones. Nothing that happens can separate us from your love, made known to us in Jesus, your beloved Son and our beloved Brother.

Psalm 56:3

Nevertheless, though I am sometimes afraid, yet put I my trust in thee.

Mark 4:40

Why are you afraid? Have you no faith?

OVERBURDENED?

O blessed Jesus Christ, who didst bid all who carry heavy burdens to come to you, refresh us with your presence and your power. Quiet our understanding and give ease to our hearts by bringing us close to things infinite and eternal. Open to us the mind of God, that in his light we may see and understand. And crown your choice of us to be your servants, by making us springs of strength and joy to all whom we serve.

Evelyn Underhill (1874–1941)

Matthew 11:28–29

Come to me all of you who are weary and overburdened and I will give you rest! Put on my yoke . . . for [it fits so easily that] my burden is light.

UNDER A DARK CLOUD

There have been times, O Lord, when I have walked the hilltops with you, when I have felt you near, and my heart has been warm in the remembrance of blessings in the past. But now . . . my heart is dry and cold, moods of depression come over me, prayer seems unreal, you seem hidden, dark clouds descend upon my spirits . . . something seems to whisper, "Keep steady, if you cannot give warmth of feeling, give your desire for me, your hunger for me, your emptiness . . . above the dark cloud, my sun is shining always . . . let quick darts of faith pierce the cloud . . . stretch out your hand in the dark . . . you will find my hand near . . . my child, my dear child!"

Psalm 139:11

Yea, the darkness is no darkness with Thee: but the night is as clear as the day: the darkness and light to Thee are both alike.

MOODS

O my Lord, when moods of depression, anxiety, or resentment take possession of me, let me ask, "Why art thou so heavy, O my soul, and why art thou so disquieted within me?"

And let the answer show me the cause of my mood and dispel it, so that I forget my hurts and want only you.

Psalm 30:5

Heaviness may endure for a night, but joy comes in the morning.

WHEN FEELING HURT

O Lord, my God, grant that when I am hurt I may open my heart to you for healing; when I feel self-willed come to you for self-noughting; when worried lay my burden at your feet, and gain from you serenity and love, O my Lord.

Jeremiah 17:14

Heal me, O Lord, that I may be healed; Save me that I may be saved: For thou art my praise.

AT MY WITS' END

Dear Lord, I am often worried and get duodenal ulcers, almost torn in two by conflicting desires and reluctance to make decisions, I get feelings of guilt though assured by others of your forgiveness. I sometimes induce ailments to escape tasks from which I shrink. I want to be loved by others, but I find others difficult to love. Heal my mind. O Father, assure me that you forgive seventy times seven, unify my mind in your will, and make me know that your grace is sufficient for every difficulty, weakness, and duty. Let me look for you in every storm, and keep my eyes on you. Then I shall walk the stormy waves, and if I sink you will stretch out your hand to rescue me, O God of my salvation.

Psalm 103:3–4

Who forgiveth all thy sin, and healeth all thine infirmities: who saveth thy life from destruction, and crowneth thee with mercy and loving kindness.

DISCONCERTING PRAYER

O God, the more I pray, the more I become conscious of the gap between your holiness and mine, your love and mine, the more I see my secret sins which I hide from others but cannot hide from you. Holy God, I have sinned against you, against others, against myself, against your Laws, against your light, against your love. Again and again, seventy times seven and more, you say to me, "Child, your sins are forgiven." O gracious, loving Lord.

Psalm 51:17

A broken and contrite heart, O God, thou will not despise. . . . Create in me a clean heart, O God, and put a new and right spirit within me.

FALLING SHORT

O righteous God, I know how far short I fall of your Law, I know how far short of your will, even more how far short of your glory, but most of all of your hope. I am not a fraction of what I can become through your grace. With Peter, I cry out, "Depart from me, for I am a sinful man, O Lord," but if you take me at my word, I shall be hopeless and heartbroken. O merciful God, O merciful Son.

Romans 3:23

All have sinned and fall short of the glory of God.

WHEN THE SPIRIT IS UNQUIET

O sabbath rest by Galilee!
　O calm of hills above,
Where Jesus knelt to share with Thee
The silence of eternity
　Interpreted by love!

Drop thy still dews of quietness,
　Till all our strivings cease;
Take from our souls the strain and stress,
And let our ordered lives confess
　The beauty of thy peace.

　　　　　J. G. Whittier (1807–92)

Isaiah 30:15

In returning and rest you shall be saved; in quietness and
in trust shall be your strength.

WHEN FAITH IS STRAINED

In times of doubts and questions, when our belief is perplexed by new learning, new teaching, new thought, when our faith is strained by creeds, by doctrines, by mysteries beyond our understanding, give us the faithfulness of learners, and the courage of believers in thee: give us boldness to examine and faith to trust all truth, stability to hold fast our tradition with enlightened interpretation, to grasp new knowledge and combine it loyally and honestly with the old; alike from stubborn rejection of new revelation and from hasty assurance that we are wiser than our fathers, save us and help us, O Lord.

Bishop Ridding

John 7:17

If any man wills to do his will, he shall know of the teaching whether it be of God.

WHEN IRRITATED

O God, I often get irritated and impatient, when people are boring, long-winded, when I can't get my own way. Sometimes I manage to suppress my irritation, but it is still there. You offer me the gift of patience, and I have a nasty feeling that soon after I have asked you for it, you will try my patience to see if I really have yours.

Psalm 139:23

Try me, O God, and seek the ground of my heart; prove me and examine my thoughts.

UNSATISFIED?

The more I win Thee, Lord,
   the more for Thee, I pine;
Ah, such a heart as mine!

My eyes behold Thee and
   are filled, and straightway then
Their hunger wakes again!

My arms have clasped Thee and
   Should set Thee free, but no,
I cannot let Thee go!

Thou dwell'st within my heart;
   forthwith anew the fire
Burns of my soul's desire.

Lord Jesus Christ, Beloved,
   tell, O tell me true,
What shall thy servant do?

              Tilak (an Indian
              Christian poet)

"I CAN'T SLEEP"

O God, I cannot get to sleep . . . when I am anxious, sad, hurt, or angry, I turn and toss, and when I do get to sleep I wake up tired. Lord, let my tired, worried spirit reach and touch you and gain something of your stillness and serenity, experience your unfailing love. And if I do not sleep I may then rest, with trust in you and good will toward your other children, O Lord of the quiet heart.

Psalm 127:2

It is in vain that you rise up early and go late to rest, eating the bread of anxious toil, for he gives to his beloved sleep.

Growing Old

FEARING OLD AGE

Creator God, when I was young I rejoiced in the health of my body, the strength of my mind, the ease of my memory. Now that I am growing old, I realize that those powers are failing, I get anxious about even small ailments, secretly I am afraid of death, I am tempted to regret retirement. God, I wish that your perfect Son had lived to old age and so shown me how to live old age. Can it be that you are hollowing me out to be filled with the spiritual and eternal? Can it be that death is our final birth into a new order of being? O Father, I want to believe that at every stage you have kept the good wine until now. Let me feel your sustaining care, and even now glimpse the good things which you plan for all your children and the happy place being prepared for me and all my loved ones by your Son Jesus Christ.

Isaiah 46:3–4

Borne by me from your birth, carried from the womb; even to your old age I am he, and to gray hairs I will carry you. I have made and ! will bear; I will carry and will save.

"NO USE TO ANYONE"

Lord, I don't seem to be of much use to anybody, I have become a burden to others; I have no freedom to do what I long to do, to be of some value to others. . . . Lord, are you suggesting that cheerful acceptance of my condition might be of some help to those who look after me, who happen to be in the next bed, those who come to see me? . . . Lord, are you even telling me that praying for others might help them . . . that distance is no obstacle . . . that even those who are now out of sight in death can be reached by the radar of love, which will come back to me as it finds them . . . that my desire and prayer can help create an aura of hope . . . even that my suffering can be the opportunity for your caress?

Luke 22:31–32

Simon, Simon, behold, Satan demanded to have you, that he might sift you like wheat, but I have prayed for you that your faith may not fail; and when you have turned again, strengthen your brethren.

WANTING TO DIE

O God, there are times when I want to die, when there seems no hope ahead, when the weaknesses of the body afflict me, when a much loved one dies. At such moments I want to end it all. But I have the fear that even that will not end it all, that the moment after will be worse than the moment before, for I shall still be unhappy with another sin on my heavy heart. Lord, take this up from me, let this temptation pass. Lord, even as I pray this desperate little prayer, I feel a little lightening of the heart, a little break in the clouds, and your love coming through.

Psalm 51:12

Gladden me with thy saving aid again, and give me a willing spirit as my strength.

MY OWN DEATH

Grant, dear Lord, that when the time comes I may believe that the moment I fall asleep here in this world I may awake there in the next world, that an immediate changeover from time to eternity takes place, that as I pass through what seems a valley of shadow I shall see the clear light of eternal day ahead, see your welcoming smile and be clasped in the ever-open arms of love, dear Father of souls.

Luke 23:43

Today, you will be with me in Paradise.

THE HEART OF A CHILD

O Christ, I am puzzled by your saying that to enter the kingdom I must become a child again. I have become set in my ways and find it hard to change. I am afraid of being thought childish. Let me remember the sense of wonder, the spontaneity, the trust, the joy of Christmas cribs and Christmas trees, the happy birthdays. O God, as I grow old let me keep young in spirit, let me rejoice in children at play, let me trust you as the Eternal Father-and-Mother, your protecting care and tender love, your never-failing hope. Father, dear Father!

Matthew 18:3

Truly, I say to you, unless you turn and become like children, you will never enter the kingdom of heaven.

Times of Trial

IN SICKNESS AND IN HEALTH

Lord, teach me the art of patience whilst I am well, and give me the use of it when I am sick. In that day either lighten my burden or strengthen my back. Make me, who so often in my health have discovered my weakness, presuming on my own strength, to be strong in my sickness when I rely solely on your assistance; through Jesus Christ, my Lord.

Thomas Fuller (1608–61)

2 Corinthians 12:9

My grace is enough for you, for my strength finds its full scope in your weakness.

HEARING BAD NEWS

O God, my heart is heavy with this bad news. You tell me that you are always at work to bring good out of evil and blessing out of misfortune. You bring good news to the heart, news of unfailing love, of forgiveness for every sin and grace for every situation, and of your invincible desire to establish your loving, right, effective rule in the hearts and affairs of men.

Psalm 112:7

He will not be afraid of any evil tidings: for his heart standeth fast and believeth in the Lord.

A FRIEND IS SICK

May the healing love of God come upon
   you, making you whole in body, mind,
   and spirit,
Assuring you of his presence ever with you,
And of his grace sufficient for your every need.

John 11:3

Lord, he whom you love is sick.

A LOVED ONE HAS DIED

We give back to you O God, those whom you gave to us. You did not lose them when you gave them to us, and we do not lose them by their return to you. Your dear Son has taught us that life is eternal and love cannot die. So death is only a horizon and a horizon is only the limit of our sight. Open our eyes to see more clearly, and draw us closer to you that we may know that we are nearer to our loved ones, who are with you. You have told us that you are preparing a place for us: prepare us also for that happy place, that where you are we may also be always, O dear Lord of life and death.

William Penn (1644–1718)

John 10:29

No one is able to snatch them out of the Father's hand.

Lord, all these years we were so close to one another, we did everything together, we seemed to know what each was feeling, without the need of words, and now she is gone. Every memory hurts. . . . Sometimes there comes a feeling that she is near, just out of sight. Sometimes I feel your reproach that to be so submerged in grief is not to notice that she is eager to keep in touch with me, as I with her. O dear Lord, I pray out of a sore heart that it may be so, daring to believe that it can be so.

John 11:35–36

Jesus wept. So they who stood by said, "See how he loved him!"

AT A FUNERAL

Eternal Lord God, grant me a glimpse of the new order of being into which your child has now entered; may he feel at home there and continue to grow in happiness, holiness, maturity, and love. I thank you that our relationships of love cannot be broken by physical death. I cannot but be sad that he is out of physical sight, yet not out of touch, for we are both in your hands and nothing harmful can hurt us. Unto your gracious mercy and protection we commit him. May he see the smile of your welcome and smile back in warm gratitude and love, O Father of souls.

1 Corinthians 2:9 and Isaiah 64:4

What no eye has seen, nor ear heard, nor the heart of man conceived, God has prepared for those who love him.

IN SUFFERING

Let the healing grace of your love, O Lord, so transform me that I may play my part in the transfiguration of the world from a place of suffering, death, and corruption to a realm of infinite light, joy, and love. Make me so obedient to your Spirit that my life may become a living prayer and a witness to your unfailing presence.

Martin Israel

Isaiah 43:2

When you pass through the water I will be with you, and through the rivers they shall not overwhelm you; when you walk through fire you shall not be burned, and the flame shall not consume you.

HOPELESS SITUATIONS

O God, nowadays we know so much about seemingly hopeless situations, fear of nuclear war, widespread hunger and disease, acts of violence, earthquakes and floods, death by cancer, despairing suicides. Lord, I hope that my prayer can somehow keep hopeless situations tied to you, so that you don't get pushed out. I long for human society to be more like the world you want, free from fear, free from want, free from pain, free from hatred and war. O Creator God, the whole of humanity is groaning in frustration and pain, longing for your completed creation. Your kingdom come! Your will be done! O just, righteous, and loving God.

Hebrews 12:26–27

Yet once more I will shake not only the earth but also the heaven . . . that what cannot be shaken may remain.

A CHILD DESPERATELY ILL

O God, whom Jesus called "Father," can you understand my anxiety? Help me to calm my aching heart; don't let my fear touch this little one. Let me believe that he is in your hand, that your love will keep him safe, whatever happens. Let my trust in you wrap him 'round with my love and yours. I entrust him to you, dear Father, trying to believe that he could be in no better hands.

2 Samuel 18:33

"O my son Absalom, my son, my son Absalom! Would I had died instead of you, O Absalom, my son, my son!"

———

CANCER DIAGNOSED

O God, I try to keep a stiff upper lip when I am with others, but secretly I am afraid; dreadfully afraid. For the moment, I am in a dark valley, a very dark valley. I know that this is where my faith and trust are being tested. I remember that your beloved and loving Son sweated blood when it seemed death was near, but prayed that the cup might pass if it should be your good and loving will. Father, I pray that prayer with him and trust with him that you will be with me and that nothing can snatch me from your hand.

Psalm 23:4

Yea, though I walk through the valley of the shadow of death, I will fear no evil.

Seeking Guidance and Strength

FEELING LOST

O my God, I have no idea where I am going. I do not
see the road ahead of me . . . nor do I really know
myself, and the fact that I think I am following your will
does not mean that I am actually doing so. But I desire
to do your will, and I know the very desire pleases you.
Therefore I will trust you always though I may seem to
be lost. I will not fear, for you are always with me, O my
dear God.

Thomas Merton (1915–)

Psalm 119:176

I have strayed like a lost sheep; come, search for thy servant.

WHICH WAY TO TURN?

Dear Lord, quiet my spirit and fix my thoughts
   on your will, that I may see what you want
   done, and contemplate its doing,
without self-consciousness,
without inner excitement,
without haste and without delay,
without fear of other people's judgments,
or anxiety about success,
knowing only that it is your will and
   must therefore be done quietly, faithfully,
   and lovingly, for in your will
alone is our peace.

Psalm 143:8

Show thou me the way that I should walk in, for I lift up my
soul unto thee.

CONSCIOUS OF FAILURE

Dear Master, in Whose life I see
All that I long and fail to be,
Let Thy clear light forever shine
To shame and guide this life of mine.

Though what I dream and what I do
In my poor days are always two,
Help me, oppressed by things undone,
O Thou, Whose dreams and deeds were one.

John Hunter (1728–93)

John 15:5

Apart from me you can do nothing.

WHY?

God, why have you done this to me? What have I
done to deserve this? . . . Lord, are you suggesting that
you did not do this? That you are in it to bring good out
of it, a good better than if this had never happened?
That you are with me to see me through? That I may
have another kind of sight, to see into the unknown, the
eternal? . . . another kind of hearing, to hear whispers of
the heart? . . . a feeling of a hand on the shoulder as of
an unseen companion? Go on, dear Lord, the why
doesn't seem to matter quite so much. . . .

Psalm 3:5–6

Why art thou so heavy, O my soul? And why art thou so disquieted within me? O put thy trust in God; for I will yet give
him thanks, which is the help of my countenance, and my
God.

STILL UNFINISHED

Creator God, I used to think that my creation was finished when I was born. I now know that the creation of a soul takes a lifetime and more. You have shown me a pattern in the human life of your dear Son, the first man as you meant him to be, the firstborn of many brothers and sisters. He is always with us in Spirit to help us to become what you want us to be, and then to work with you in creating the kind of world you want. O help me to keep myself under your creating hands and to open my whole being to your incarnation.

Ephesians 4:13

So we shall all at last attain . . . to mature manhood, measured by nothing less than the full stature of Christ.

Psalm 63:2

My soul thirsts for Thee, my flesh also longs for Thee, like a barren and dry land where no water is.

A COMMITTED DISCIPLE?

O God, there has never been anyone quite like Jesus, who knows you so intimately, who is so open to your inspiration, who loves people as you do, who shares your plans, yet knows us humans because he is one of us. O God, I thank you for him, I come to you through him, I will try to grow like him, I will enlist under him to work for the world you want, and to bring your love and blessing into every single life, O God and Father of Jesus Christ.

John 6:66–67

After this many of his disciples drew back and no longer went about with him. Jesus said to the twelve, "Will you also go away?" Simon Peter answered him, "Lord, to whom shall we go? You have the words of eternal life."

Relationships with Other People

IN BITTERNESS

O Lord God, my heart is bitter. I cannot yet forgive the hurt done to me, but I know that I can pour out my heart to you in all its bitterness. I know also that this root of bitterness can become a cancer in the soul. I know further that unless I forgive others, I go outside the circle of your forgiving compassion and love. Soften my heart, dear Father, with your healing grace and number me with your forgiving Son, who found excuse for those who nailed him to the cross.

Psalm 142:2

I pour out my complaint before him, I tell my trouble before him.

FEELING ANGRY

O God, your perfect Son was a man of strong
feelings, in the desecration of your house, in the
hypocrisies of his critics, in the slowness of heart of his
disciples, in the damage that sin was doing to your
children. I too burn with anger, not a warm
compassionate anger like his, but one that spills over
into hurting, retaliation, and sin. Forgive me, holy,
righteous Father, and grant that I may oppose all evil
with your forgiving compassion and love.

Ephesians 4:26

Be angry but do not sin; do not let the sun go down on your
anger.

THE NEED TO BE LOVED

Lord God, we your human children are learning from experience that we must have love; without it we go wrong. We see how little ones without the warm love of father and mother never really recover. Every soul cries out, "I want to be loved." Lord, it takes a lot of faith to think that out of billions of souls you love each one, as if he were an only child. Nothing can kill your love for me . . . nothing I do, whatever happens to me, wherever I go, even in the hells I make for myself. O Father-and-Mother God.

Jeremiah 31:3

I have loved you with an everlasting love.

THE NEED TO LOVE

O God, I find your command to love everyone difficult. There are so many unlovable people. You even say that we must love those who hate us and do us harm. As my heart talks to you about this, you remind me that there is something more important—to love you first. Your beloved and loving Son tells us that we shall love when we realize you love us. You love every single soul. Your love creates love. Loving Lord, make me loving toward him . . . toward her . . . toward them . . . toward everyone. Father of love, give me this best gift of all . . . the ability to love!

1 John 3:14

We know that we have passed out of death into life, because we love the brethren.

THE WORLD'S PAIN

O Lord,
    so many sick
    so many starving
    so many deprived
    so many sad
    so many bitter
    so many fearful.
When I look at them
    my heart fails.
When I look at you
    I hope again.
Help me to help you
    to reduce the world's pain
O God of infinite Compassion
    O ceaseless Energy of Love.

Psalm 145:9

The Lord is loving unto every man; and his mercy is over
all his works.

BREAKING MARRIAGES

God, whose eternal mind
  Rules the round world over,
Whose wisdom lies behind
  All that men discover:
Grant that they, by thought and speech,
May grow nearer each to each;
  Lord, let sweet converse bind
    Lover unto lover.
      Bless them, God of loving.

God, whose unbound grace
  Heaven and earth pervadeth
Whose mercy doth embrace
  All thy wisdom madeth.
Grant that they may, hand in hand,
All forgive, all understand;
  Keeping, through time and space,
    Trust that never fadeth.
      Bless them, God of loving.

Jan Struther (1901–53)

Ruth 1:16–17

Where you go I will go, and where you lodge I will lodge;
your people shall be my people, and your God my God;
where you die I will die, and there will I be buried. May the
Lord do so to me and more also if even death parts me from
you.

FOR MEN OF VIOLENCE

O Lord

Remember not only the men and women of good will
but also those of ill will.

Do not only remember the suffering they have inflicted
on us, remember the fruits we brought, thanks to this
suffering, our comradeship, our loyalty, our humility,
the courage, the generosity, the greatness of heart
which has grown out of all this.

And when they come to judgment, let all the fruits we
have borne be their forgiveness.

> Found on a piece of wrapping paper,
> near the body of a dead child, in
> Ravensbrück Nazi Concentration Camp.
> Quoted in Martin Israel,
> *The Pain That Heals*, p. 113

Luke 23:34

Father, forgive them; for they know not what they do.

For Thyself Alone

THYSELF ALONE

O my God, if I worship Thee in desire for heaven, exclude me from heaven; if I worship Thee for fear of hell, burn me in hell. But if I worship thee for Thyself alone, then withhold not from me thine eternal beauty.

Rabi'a (a Muslim woman saint who lived in Jerusalem circa A.D. 800)

Rumi, a Persian poet (1207–73)

The lovers of God have no religion but God alone.

NEVER ENOUGH

Lord, my heart is not large enough,
   my memory is not good enough,
   my will is not strong enough.
Take my heart and enlarge it,
Take my memory and give it quicker recall
   of your mercies and my failing.
Take my will and strengthen it,
   and make me conscious of you
     ever present
     ever guiding
     never failing
      always loving,
       Blessed Lord.

Isaiah 57:15

For thus says the high and lofty One who inhabits eternity, whose name is Holy: "I dwell in the high and holy place, and also with him who is of a contrite and humble spirit."

THE ETERNAL MYSTERY

O God, your immensity fills the earth and the whole universe, but the universe itself cannot contain you, much less the earth and still less the world of my thoughts.

Fr. Yves Raguin

St. Augustine

O Thou Supreme! most secret and most present, most beautiful and strong! What shall I say, my God, my Life, my Holy Joy? What shall any man say when he speaks of Thee?

Prayers from a Pastoral Heart

BAPTISM I

O Father, what will this child be ten, twenty, thirty and more years on, with these parents, godparents, this congregation, and me your unworthy priest? I know your love for each child. Grant that it may be ours too.

BAPTISM II

O God, by whose providence human love is permitted to create new life, we want this little one to have your grace throughout his life, his parents to make his home a home of love, his godparents to watch over his true welfare, so that as year follows year, he may be surrounded by love and grow like your perfect Son, blessed by you and a joy to all who know him. We know this is your will for him, O Father of all.

Luke 1:66

"What then will this child be?" For the hand of the Lord is with him.

CONFIRMATION I

O Holy Spirit, you know the hearts of these standing before you today. You know what has brought them here. Lord, I think they know their need to be made strong for all the difficulties, temptations, and adventures of life. O Father, may they turn to you at every step and feel the hand of your perfect Son Jesus on their shoulder, accompanying, guiding, blessing them.

CONFIRMATION II

Dear Lord, you looked with love on the eager young man who wanted your quality of life. I know you look with the same love on these young and old who promise to turn to you in every situation of life, who realize their need to be made strong. Keep them traveling along with you in the adventure of life, in all its opportunities and difficulties. Grant that my life may be a support to them, and their dedication inspire a renewal of mine, O perfect brother of us all, O perfect Son of the Eternal Father.

Philippians 4:13
I can do all things in him who strengthens me.

CELEBRATING THE EUCHARIST

O Christ, this is your Eucharist, and these your people come to be fed with heavenly food. Don't let my unworthiness hinder your grace, but let me forget myself in the wonder of your ever-present love.

AT A WEDDING

O Holy Spirit, remind me that today is the happiest day so far in the lives of this couple, who come to give themselves to each other, and to ask your blessing and grace. Grant that with your presence in their married life every succeeding day may be even happier. Let joy and faith shine through my part in this sacrament of human love and divine grace.

PREACHING

O Eternal Word, give me a word from you, to touch the hearts of those who hope and trust in you and . . . in me, your representative. Don't let me cover it with too many words of mine. Don't let me be afraid of what they will think of me. Let the way I say it convince them that it comes from you, to me as well as to them.

TOO BUSY

O God, she said that she hesitated to come to me because I always seemed so busy. Forgive me, Lord. Make me know that the care and cure of souls must be my most important work, and give me your love for everyone whom you know by name, and love as if each were your only care.

DECLARING GOD'S FORGIVENESS

O Ever-Merciful God, grant that the assurance of your unceasing forgiveness may melt my heart to penitence, gratitude and love, and that this assurance may win the hearts of all in my care, and bring them to the longing, welcoming, embracing love of your Sacred Heart.

WITH THE DYING

O Lover of Souls, grant me your eternal love, as I stand by the bedside of the dying. Without your love, I am at the best only doing my duty. Speak through my words and through my silence, through your delegated love, a word of comfort, trust, and expectant hope and joy. O home of every heart.

BEFORE A FUNERAL

O Ever-living Christ, don't let me be just a functional priest, but one also who believes with you the Father's will of continuing life and love, the assurance of forgiveness and the hope of continuing growth in love and holiness.

PRAYING THE PRAYERS

O God, so often when I am praying with your people, my thoughts are on making myself heard, or almost preaching to them, rather than on lifting my heart and theirs to you. I often recite the prayers rather than pray them. Let your spirit pray within me and in them, that we may be a praying, worshiping people, offering ourselves for your wise and gracious will for us and all your children, through Christ your ever-blessed and ever-blessing Son.

O God, grant your grace and love that I may stand before your people on behalf of you, and stand before you on behalf of them.

Arrow Prayers
Short prayers in time of need

For times when I feel too sick . . . too much in pain . . .
too weak . . . when eyesight is failing . . . when memory
is not as good as it once was. . . . These short prayers
sent up to God in a second of time might well be
prayed and memorized while I am well, sinking them, as
it were, deep into the heart, the very core of my being,
so that when I become ill, my deep self may remember
and pray them. Any one of them could become a tried
and trusted anchor-hold on God.

Father, dear Father!

Always in your hands, dear God.

Lord, I know that you love me.

Lord, you know I love you.

Thank you, Lord, for the loving care I receive.

Always when I think of Thee
New hope and trust spring up in me.

Though I am sometimes afraid, yet I put my trust in
Thee.

Nothing can separate me from you.

Jesus, the very thought of thee . . .

Jesus, Living Lord, you are with me,
Until the end of time . . . and beyond.

Jesus, dear brother, I follow you to God.

In my spirit's ear
Whisper, I am near.

Just as I am, I come.

Lord, you have carried me up till now,
A few steps more, dear Lord.

"It is I, be not afraid!"

Ready, Lord, for my birth into the eternal.

Into your hands, dear Lord, into your hands.

God be in my head and in my understanding.
God be in my eyes and in my looking.
God be in my mouth and in my speaking.
God be at my end and at my departing.